HOME FIREARM SAFETY

**Guidelines for
Handling and Storing
Guns in the Home**

First Edition—June 1990
© 1990 The National Rifle Association of America

ES5N1204   1-93

C O N T E N T S

INTRODUCTION

The purpose of this book is to introduce the basic principles of firearm safety. It concentrates on gun handling and storage *within the home*.

Guns are neither safe nor unsafe by themselves. When people practice responsible ownership and use, firearms are safe. The number of accidental firearm fatalities has dropped 52 percent between 1967 and 1988, according to National Safety Council surveys (Appendix 1). This decline is a direct result of the increase and effectiveness of gun safety programs.

The National Rifle Association has promoted firearm education and marksmanship training for more than 100 years. NRA's concern for public safety led to support of the earliest hunter education courses and continues today through many gun safety and training programs. But all of us share the responsibility for learning what firearm safety involves. With guns found in about half of all American homes today, gun owners as well as non-gun owners should know gun safety.

Upon finishing this book, the reader should understand and be able to apply:

- The basic elements of gun safety — attitude, knowledge and skill;
- The fundamental rules of safe gun handling;
- How to identify and unload different types of firearms;
- The different types and uses of ammunition;
- How to clean and care for guns;
- Factors for evaluating gun storage options.

Understanding these points will enable the reader to enjoy the many benefits of gun ownership and participation in shooting activities.

WHY WE OWN GUNS

Nearly 70 million Americans own firearms and enjoy their safe and positive uses. Guns provide us with the means to participate in a variety of recreational, competitive and educational pursuits. Nearly 18 million people in this country hunt. Millions more enjoy competition and recreational shooting, gun collecting, and historical reenactment. Guns are tools for personal protection, and they are the elements upon which

popular collegiate and Olympic sports are centered. People from all walks of life own guns and participate in shooting sports. Many people become involved in shooting at a young age and stay active throughout their lives. Guns offer American society a vast opportunity for shared experiences—as long as we share the responsibility to learn and diligently apply safe gun handling practices.

CHAPTER 1

THE ELEMENTS OF GUN SAFETY

None of us would allow someone to be injured if it could be prevented. The fact of the matter is, accidental gun injuries can be prevented by accepting responsibility and taking the necessary actions. We are responsible for gun safety!

Home accidents involving guns generally result from one of two causes: ignorance or carelessness. The three basic elements of gun safety—positive attitude, knowledge, and skill—eliminate both causes. Understanding the meaning of these elements is the first step toward accepting responsibility for gun safety.

A positive attitude is the *most* important element in gun safety; it is simply a matter of accepting the responsibility to act safely. It is a mental awareness that safety is always first and foremost when dealing with guns.

Knowledge means knowing and understanding the gun safety rules and how to apply them to any situation. It is knowing how guns and ammunition operate and how to handle them correctly. Knowledge is also being aware of what you do not know and when or where to go for help.

Skill in handling firearms safely means actually applying the gun safety rules. Skill is perfected through practice.

FUNDAMENTAL GUN SAFETY RULES

There are three fundamental rules of gun safety. These rules apply when handling any gun under any circumstances:

1. Always Keep the Gun Pointed in a Safe Direction.
2. Always Keep Your Finger Off the Trigger Until You Are Ready to Shoot.
3. Always Keep the Gun Unloaded Until Ready to Use.

These rules are general and can be applied in a variety of ways. It is important to understand how each rule fits various situations.

1

This is the golden rule of gun safety. A "safe direction" means that the gun is pointed so that even if it were to go off it would not cause injury. The key to this rule is to control where the muzzle or front end of the barrel is pointed at all times. Common sense dictates the safest direction, depending on different circumstances.

For example, if you are outside, it is generally safe to point a gun up or down. However, inside the home, some judgment is involved. If you are on the bottom floor, don't point the gun up since a shot could go through the ceiling to a room above. If you are upstairs, don't point the gun down, since a shot might penetrate the floor. Regardless of where you are, always be aware of where the gun is pointing and what is beyond. Naturally, safety demands that a gun never be pointed at another person.

> **Rule #2**: Always Keep Your Finger Off the Trigger Until Ready to Shoot.

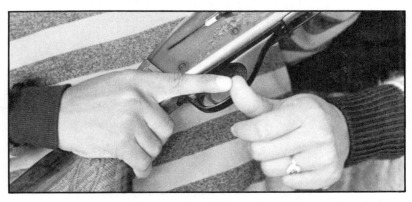

When holding a gun, people have a natural tendency to place their finger on the trigger. *Don't do it!* Rest your finger on the trigger guard or along the side of the gun. Until you are actually ready to fire, do not touch the trigger.

This rule is particularly important in the home, where guns are sometimes shown to or handled by visitors.

> **Rule #3**: Always Keep the Gun Unloaded Until Ready to Use.

Whenever you pick up a gun, immediately open the action and look into the rear of the gun's barrel. This area is known as the chamber and should be clear of ammunition. (If the gun has a magazine, remove it before opening the action and make sure it is empty.) If you do not know how to open the action, leave the gun alone and get help from someone who does. Guns do not all operate the same way, and procedures for opening the actions are not standard. Guns usually have an owner's manual that explains how to operate a specific model. *Read that manual and understand it before attempting to handle the firearm.* If you still do not feel comfortable, seek help from a person trained to handle firearms.

The phrase "ready for use" needs some explanation. A gun kept in the home for protection is essentially always in use and may be kept loaded if special care is taken. The gun must be stored in a secure place, inaccessible to unauthorized users (children or adults) and in accordance with local laws. As a general rule, guns used for any purpose other than personal protection should never be loaded in the home. Guns used for hunting and competition, for example, are not ready for use until the hunter reaches the field or the target shooter steps to the firing line.

SPECIAL RESPONSIBILITIES FOR PARENTS

Parents who own guns have a special responsibility to practice safe gun handling. Be positive role models and talk openly about safety practices. The worst danger comes when a child considers guns a taboo or mystery that should be investigated when alone. The parent must, through example as well as instruction, set guidelines for children to follow.

Deciding when a child is old enough to receive training for any potentially dangerous situation can be difficult. The first time a child shows an interest in guns, regardless of age, is a signal that some type of safety training is necessary. The child may simply ask a question or act out "gun play." He or she has probably already seen examples of unsafe gun handling on television, in the movies, or in toy gun battles with his or her friends. The point here is that a child's gun safety training should begin as soon as he or she shows an interest in guns.

The type of safety training that should be taught depends on the maturity of the child.* A parent's earliest guidelines may allow the child to touch a gun, but only with permission and only if a parent is present. An older child may be allowed to hold a gun, under adult supervision, while keeping the muzzle pointed in a safe direction. Should the child come across a gun without a parent present, he or she should be taught to:

STOP—DON'T TOUCH
LEAVE THE AREA
TELL AN ADULT

Parents also need to make sure that a child understands the difference between pretend and real life. They need to explain that shootings seen on television are "pretend"; they do not reflect real life. Never assume a child knows the difference.

---

*Gun safety training material designed for children in kindergarten through the sixth grade is available from NRA. See the resources list in the appendices for ordering information.

CHAPTER 2

Virtually any accident involving a gun can be prevented if a person accepts and practices the responsibility of learning safe gun handling rules and understanding how guns operate. **However, the operation of different guns varies, and it is essential to read the owner's manual and understand it before attempting to unload a particular gun. Should you have any questions about how a firearm operates, do not experiment! Consult a knowledgeable individual for assistance.**

TYPES OF FIREARMS

There are three basic types of firearms—handguns, rifles and shotguns. These may be identified by their various actions. The term "action" refers to the group of parts through which ammunition for that gun is loaded, fired and unloaded. Handgun actions are sometimes different than those found on rifles and shotguns. A handgun has a shorter barrel and a grip instead of a stock (for holding it in the hand). Rifles and shotguns are similar in how their actions operate and both have long barrels and stocks. The major difference between rifles and shotguns is that they fire different types of ammunition.

HANDGUNS

Some people, because of a lack of knowledge, consider handguns to be dangerous. However, handguns may be handled just as safely as rifles or shotguns by trained individuals. Today, more than ever before, people are discovering the usefulness of handguns for personal protection and recreation. This fact alone makes it especially important to understand how handguns operate, thereby reducing the possibility of an accident. The first step in understanding how a firearm operates is to understand the different types. The two most common types of handguns are revolvers and semi-automatics.

Most people are familiar with the general appearance of revolvers. They are often seen in Westerns and in various police and detective television programs. A revolver has a cylinder that holds the ammunition and revolves as the gun's hammer is cocked or as the trigger is pulled.

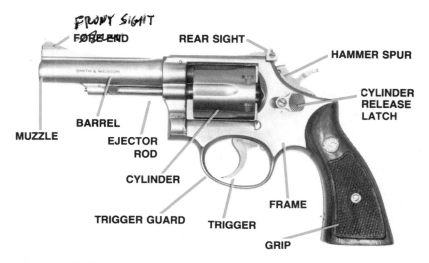

FRONT SIGHT
FOREND   REAR SIGHT
                        HAMMER SPUR

                        CYLINDER
                        RELEASE
                        LATCH

BARREL
MUZZLE
    EJECTOR
    ROD

CYLINDER

                    FRAME

TRIGGER GUARD   TRIGGER

            GRIP

The cylinder is loaded by inserting cartridges, one into each hole, or chamber. The cartridge is then ready to fire as the cylinder rotates, aligning each loaded chamber with the barrel. On a single-action revolver, the hammer must be pulled before each shot to rotate the cylinder and align the next chamber with the barrel. On a double-action revolver, pulling the trigger cocks the hammer, rotates the cylinder to its proper alignment, and fires the shot, all in one movement. Double action means that the trigger performs two functions—to cock and fire the gun.

To check that a double-action revolver is unloaded:

1. Point the gun in a safe direction.
2. Keep your finger off the trigger.

3. Activate the cylinder release latch and swing the cylinder out for visual

inspection. If cartridges are in the cylinder, point the muzzle up, push the ejector rod to the rear, and catch the cartridges in your hand.

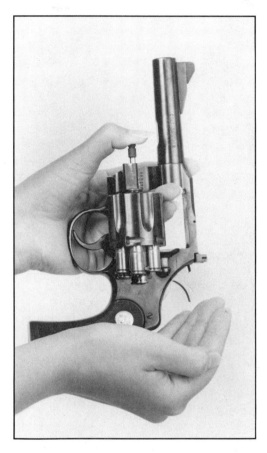

The single-action revolver does not permit you to inspect all chambers at once. Instead, a loading gate on the side of the revolver, behind the cylinder, opens and permits you to look into the chambers one at a time.

To check a single-action revolver:

1. Point the gun in a safe direction.

2. Keep your finger off the trigger.

3. Draw the hammer back one or two clicks as required. (See owner's manual.) This releases the cylinder, allowing it to be turned freely.

4. After the loading gate is opened, the chambers may be inspected one by one. If cartridges are in the cylinder, push each out, from the front of the cylinder, using the ejector rod.

Semi-automatic handguns work differently than revolvers. A semi-automatic firearm instantly reloads and recocks itself with each pull of the trigger after the first shot is fired and will continue to do so until the magazine is empty.

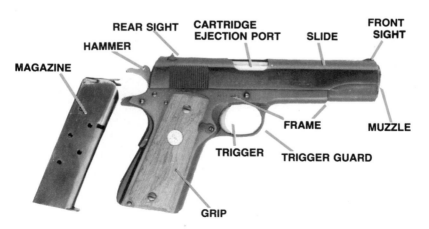

The cartridges to be fed into the chamber are stored in a magazine that is usually located within the grip. Either a button or catch releases the magazine for removal and inspection. The action is usually opened by pulling the slide on top of the gun to the rear. The action can usually be locked open with a catch located on the frame under the slide. Check the owner's manual for proper operation.

To check a semi-automatic:

1. Point the gun in a safe direction.

2. Keep your finger off the trigger.

3. Remove the magazine.

4. Holding the grip of the gun in one hand, grasp the slide firmly with the free hand and pull it back.

5. Lock the slide in the rear position, if possible.

6. If the slide cannot be locked open, either hold it back or block it with an object such as a large eraser, a clothespin or a small piece of wood.

7. Visually inspect the chamber, if possible. If there is no cartridge in the chamber, and the magazine has been removed, the gun is unloaded. If visual inspection is not possible, manually inspect the gun by inserting your little finger into the chamber.

Some semi-automatics require the magazine to be in the gun or the slide will not lock open. If this is the case, empty the cartridges from the magazine and replace it so that the slide can be locked back and held open.

There are also bolt action and hinge action handguns, which operate on the same principle as their rifle and shotgun counterparts.

RIFLES

Rifles are technically similar to handguns in some ways, but their appearance differs greatly. A rifle has a much longer barrel and the "handle" by which it is held is called the stock. The most common rifle actions are: bolt action, lever action, pump action and semi-automatic.

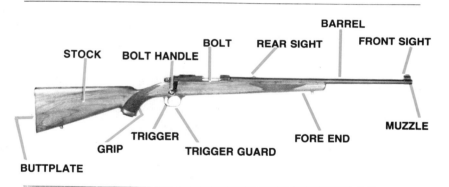

Bolt Action

A bolt action rifle operates much like an old-fashioned door bolt. Generally, there is a magazine located within the stock, or under the action, and in front of the trigger guard.

To check a bolt action rifle:

1. Point the gun in a safe direction.

2. Keep your finger off the trigger.

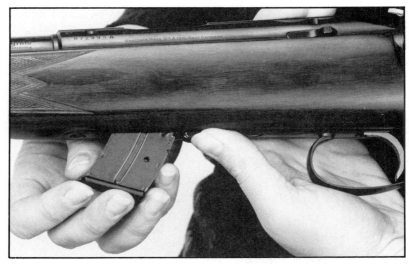

3. Remove the magazine if it can be removed. (NOTE: If the gun has a tubular magazine, see "Guns with Tubular Magazines," at the end of this section.)

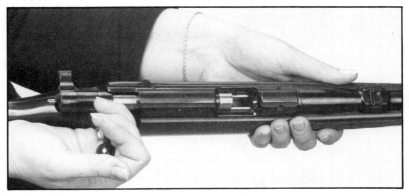

4. Open the action by lifting the bolt handle upward and then pulling it back toward you. When the action is open, the rifle cannot fire.

5. Visually inspect the chamber if possible. If not, manually inspect it by inserting your little finger into the chamber.

6. Leave the action open.

Some rifles have magazines that detach easily and some have internal magazines. The latter sometimes have a hinged floor plate or trap door on the bottom that allows the ammunition to drop out.

To check bolt actions with a hinged floor plate:

1. Point the gun in a safe direction.
2. Keep your finger off the trigger.
3. Release the floor plate to open the magazine.

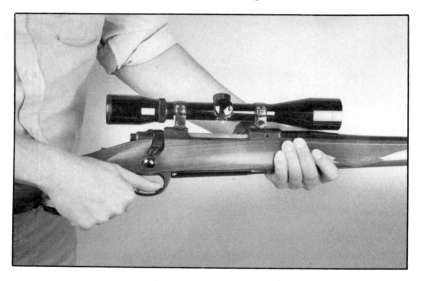

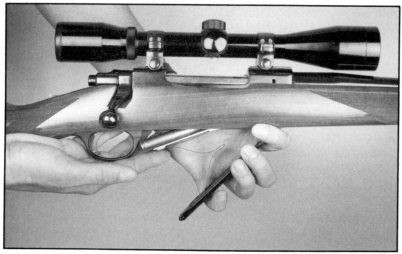

4. Catch falling cartridges in your hand.

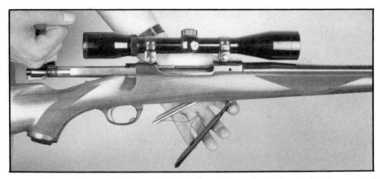

5. Open the action by lifting the bolt handle and pulling it back toward you.

6. Visually and/or manually inspect the chamber.

7. Return the floor plate to the locked position.

8. Leave the action open.

To check bolt actions with an internal magazine and no hinged floor plate:

1. Point the gun in a safe direction.

2. Keep your finger off the trigger.

3. Open and *partially* close the action. Make certain that any cartridge which may have been in the chamber is ejected. Visually and/or manually inspect the chamber to make certain.

4. *Partially* close the bolt, which should move a cartridge *part of the way* into the chamber.

5. Pull the bolt back, reach into the action and remove the cartridge. Repeat the cycle until you have removed all the cartridges.

6. Visually and/or manually inspect the chamber.

7. Leave the action open.

NOTE: If you are uncertain how to remove or release the magazine on any bolt action rifle, the gun may be unloaded in the following manner:

1. Point the gun in a safe direction.

2. Keep your finger off the trigger.

3. Open the action. Make certain that any cartridge which may have been

in the chamber is ejected. Visually and/or manually inspect the chamber to make certain.

4. *Partially* close the bolt, which should move a cartridge *part of the way* into the chamber.

5. Pull the bolt back, reach into the action and remove the cartridge. Repeat the cycle until you have removed all cartridges.

6. Visually and/or manually inspect the chamber.

7. Leave the action open.

Lever Action

Lever action rifles are popular with hunters and are commonly seen in Western movies and TV shows. Many are still manufactured today. By moving the lever forward and back, you mechanically move cartridges from the magazine (usually a tube directly under the barrel) into the chamber for firing. To check a lever action rifle:

1. Point the gun in a safe direction.

2. Keep your finger off the trigger.

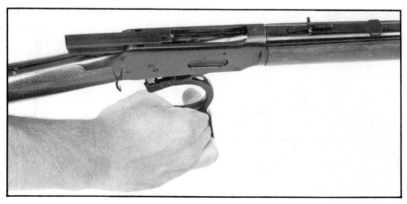

3. Push the lever down and away from you, opening the action. The gun cannot be fired with the action open.

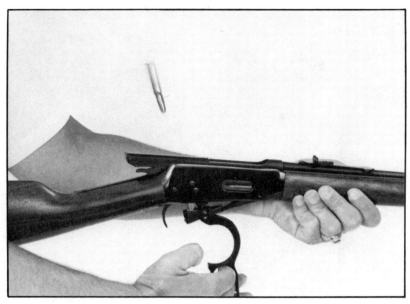

4. Work the lever until all cartridges are ejected, then visually and/or manually inspect the chamber.

5. Leave the action open. (NOTE: See "Guns with Tubular Magazines," at the end of this section.)

Some lever action rifles have detachable magazines. Even after removing the magazine, you must still open the action and make sure the chamber is empty.

Pump Action

Pump action rifles have a fore-end under the barrel that is "pumped" back and forth to operate the action. To check a pump action rifle:

1. Point the gun in a safe direction.
2. Keep your finger off the trigger.

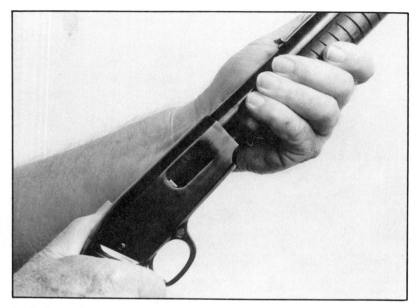

3. Pull the fore-end back toward you to open the action. A release device, usually near the trigger guard, may need to be pressed if the action has been closed and the rifle has not been fired. When the action is open, the rifle cannot be fired.

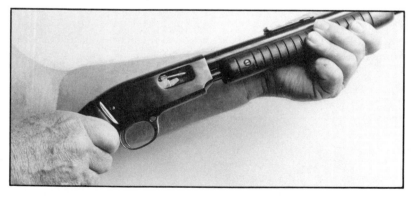

4. Work the action repeatedly until no more cartridges are ejected. Make sure the chamber is empty.

5. Even then, care must be exercised, and the action should remain open whenever the rifle is handled. (NOTE: See "Guns with Tubular Magazines," at the end of this section.)

Semi-Automatic

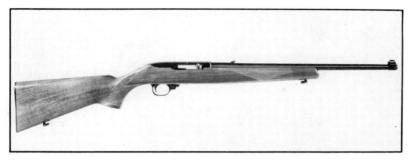

Most semi-automatic rifles have either a detachable magazine or a magazine tube, which may be under the barrel or housed within the stock.

To check a semi-automatic rifle with a detachable magazine:

1. Point the gun in a safe direction.
2. Keep your finger off the trigger.
3. Remove the magazine.

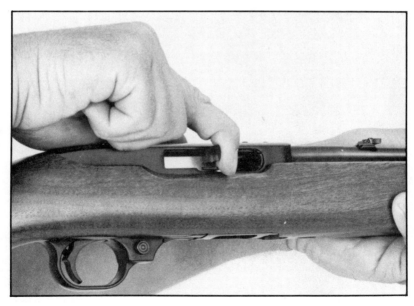

4. Pull the bolt back to open the action, and lock it open. If the action

will not lock open, insert a small piece of wood into the chamber.

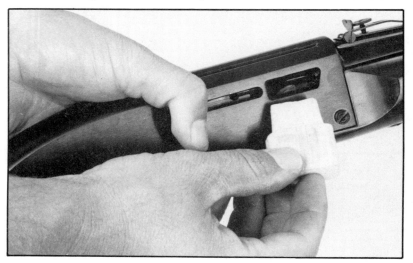

5. Visually or manually check the chamber and magazine to ensure that the rifle is unloaded.

To check a semi-automatic rifle with a tubular magazine:

1. Point the gun in a safe direction.

2. Keep your finger off the trigger.

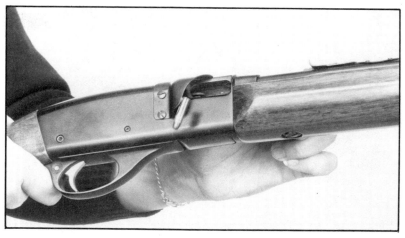

3. Pull the bolt back; a cartridge will eject if a round was chambered.

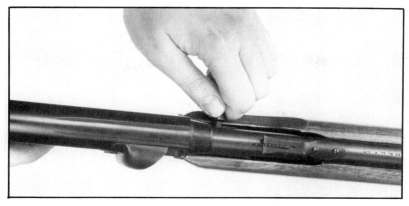

4. Gently release the bolt, which will spring forward and chamber another round.

5. Continue to pull and release the bolt until all cartridges are ejected.

6. Lock or block the bolt open and visually and/or manually inspect the chamber. (NOTE: See "Guns with Tubular Magazines," at the end of this section.)

7. Leave the action open.

SHOTGUNS

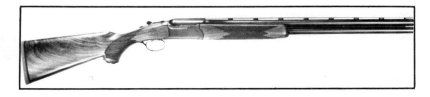

Shotguns are similar to rifles in appearance and the way their actions operate. Pump action, hinge action, and semi-automatic shotguns are the most common. There are also bolt and lever action shotguns but they are not as common. Shotguns with bolt, pump, semi-automatic, or lever actions operate the same way as rifles, although individual features may vary.

To check a hinge or break action shotgun:

1. Point the gun in a safe direction.

2. Keep your finger off the trigger.

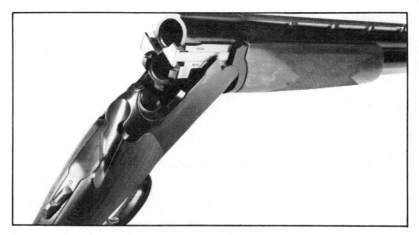

3. Push the lever, usually on top of the firearm, to the right to open the action. On many guns, shells will eject immediately.

4. Inspect the chamber, or chambers if the gun has multiple barrels.

5. If loaded, pull the shells out by hand.

6. Leave the action open.

Regardless of the type of firearm—handgun, rifle or shotgun—knowing how to check whether it is loaded or unloaded is fundamental to gun safety. In addition to the general guidelines here, always read the owner's manual for your gun before attempting to handle it. If you have any questions about how a firearm operates, do not experiment; ask a knowledgeable individual for help.

Guns with Tubular Magazines

Both shotguns and rifles, whether they have bolt, lever, pump or semi-automatic actions, may have tubular magazines. When unloading any gun with a tubular magazine, it is especially important to leave the action open even after determining that the chamber is clear. Potential exists for cartridges to get stuck within the magazine tube, creating a false impression that all the shells have been ejected. As long as the action is open, however, a cartridge cannot be moved into the chamber.

With the action open and the muzzle pointed in a safe direction, the magazine tube can be unscrewed, pulled out and cartridges removed. Caution: In some tubular magazines, a cartridge may still remain. Therefore, completely repeat the unloading sequence to double-check then block the action open at the end of the procedure.

Muzzleloading Firearms

Muzzleloaders are the predecessors of cartridge firearms; they are so named because they are loaded through the muzzle. Muzzleloading firearms are loaded with "black powder," a term describing the *type* of powder, not just the *color*. Black powder is volatile; it must be handled with special care and always kept away from heat or flame.

To load these guns, powder is poured through the muzzle into the barrel and a lead projectile is placed on top of the powder. A hole located at the rear of the barrel, just above the trigger, allows a flame or spark to enter the barrel, ignite the powder, and fire the gun.

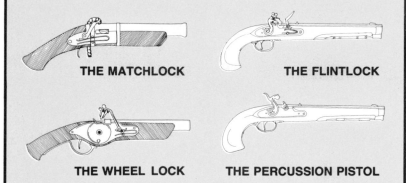

THE MATCHLOCK · THE FLINTLOCK · THE WHEEL LOCK · THE PERCUSSION PISTOL

The matchlock, one of the earliest forms of muzzleloading firearms, uses a wick-like piece of material that is lit before the gun is fired. When the trigger is pulled, the "match" is lowered into a priming pan, igniting the powder. Another version called the wheel lock has a flint and a spinning wheel that replaces the "match" by sparking and igniting the powder. Wheel locks work much like today's cigarette lighters. On flintlock muzzleloaders, a spark is created when the hammer, containing a piece of flint, strikes a metal plate or frizzen. On "percussion" muzzleloaders, the spark is produced by the hammer's striking a percussion cap. Muzzleloading handguns, rifles and shotguns are all available today. They are popular with collectors and are used in hunting, competition, recreational shooting and historical reenactments.

It is difficult to determine if a muzzleloader is loaded, and it is possible for a gun to remain loaded for many years. If you suspect a muzzleloading gun is loaded, do not attempt to handle it or try to unload it yourself. Leave it alone, secure it, and have a knowledgeable individual make sure it is unloaded.

Air Guns

BB and pellet guns, also called air guns, are especially popular as "starter guns" for young people and are commonly found in the home. They are also used in various competitions, including the Olympics, as well as for informal recreational shooting.

BB and pellet guns are very similar to cartridge firearms (rifles and pistols), except that they use springs, compressed air or carbon dioxide gas, rather than gunpowder, to propel a projectile. Although air guns are generally less powerful than cartridge firearms, they are not toys and must be used within the same guidelines as firearms. They demand responsible use and the observance of all gun safety rules.

Air gun actions also differ from those on firearms. They are typically loaded by inserting a BB or a pellet into a loading port or the rear end of the barrel.

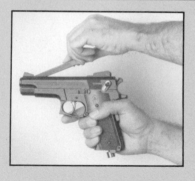

The basic procedure to tell whether a BB or pellet gun is loaded is:

- Point the gun in a safe direction.
- Keep your finger off the trigger.
- Open the loading port.
- Inspect the chamber area.

The location and operation of the loading port, however, varies widely from model to model. Refer to the owner's manual for procedures to check a specific model.

A BB or pellet gun can be unloaded by having a trained individual fire it at a safe backstop or into a container filled with several inches of newspaper. Many BB and pellet guns can be unloaded without firing, but individual differences in guns make it essential to consult the owner's manual first. The following steps give a general idea of the procedure on some types of guns. They are not intended to explain any specific model.

- Point the gun in a safe direction.
- Keep your finger off the trigger.
- Remove the magazine, if it is present and detachable.
- If the magazine is internal, open the loading port and pour out the remaining projectiles, always being certain the muzzle is pointed in a safe direction and your finger is off the trigger.
- Sight through the bore from the rear end, making sure no projectiles are lodged in the barrel. If this is not possible, pass a cleaning rod completely through the bore.

CHAPTER 3

TYPES OF AMMUNITION

Basically, a firearm is a device that holds and fires ammunition and directs the bullet or shot in the direction in which it is pointed. Ammunition varies in size and appearance and is always designed to fit in a particular size and type of gun.

RIFLE AND HANDGUN AMMUNITION

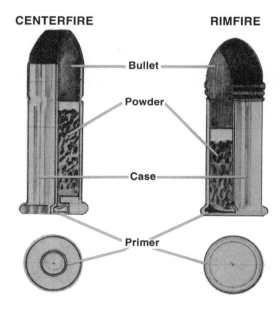

CENTERFIRE   **RIMFIRE**

Bullet

Powder

Case

Primer

Rifles and handguns use "cartridge" ammunition. A cartridge consists of four basic parts: a metal case, a primer, a powder charge and a projectile. There are two basic types of modern cartridges — "rimfire" and "centerfire." These names refer to the location of the primer. (The primer's function is explained in the section on firing sequence, at the end of this chapter.) In a rimfire cartridge, a chemical primer is located around the inside bottom rim of the case, and the bottom of the cartridge is smooth. In centerfire ammunition, the primer is located in the center of the case bottom.

In this country, ammunition is measured in caliber, which is the diameter of the bullet, usually measured in hundredths of an inch. A .22 caliber bullet is 22/100ths of an inch. (Some popular calibers are also measured in millimeters.) With the exception of rimfire cartridges, the caliber of ammunition is almost always stamped on the cartridge and *must* match a similar stamp on the firearm in which it is to be used. (Rimfire ammunition is labeled only on the box.) If the wrong ammunition is used in a firearm, serious damage or injury can result. Therefore, always remember the following rule:

Use only the correct ammunition for your gun.

SHOTGUN AMMUNITION

Shotgun ammunition is referred to as a shotgun shell. A shotgun shell consists of five parts: a case, usually made of plastic and reinforced by a metal base, a primer, a powder charge, shot (a number of pellets),

SHOTSHELL PARTS

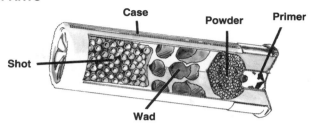

Case

Powder

Primer

Shot

Wad

and the wad, a component that separates the powder from the shot. Shot pellets come in a variety of sizes. Some shells may contain a single large projectile called a "slug." Modern shotgun shells are all centerfire.

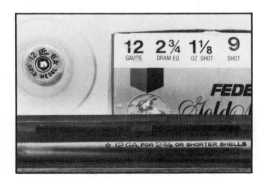

Shotgun shells, like cartridges, come in a variety of sizes (referred to as gauge) and are various lengths. The gauge and length are usually marked somewhere on the case and must match the gauge stamped on the shotgun.

FIRING SEQUENCE

Besides knowing how a firearm operates, it is helpful to understand the ammunition firing sequence. The actual sequence of events that occurs when ammunition is fired is basically the same in both cartridges and shotgun shells:

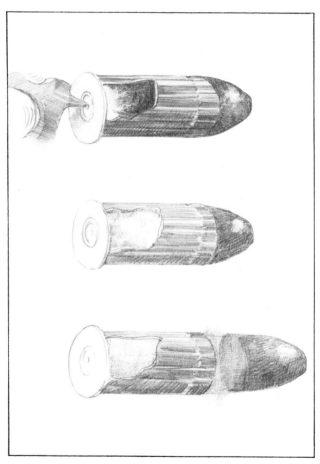

- The firing pin strikes and detonates the primer.
- The primer ignites the powder, which through burning, produces gases.
- The expanding gases push the projectile through the barrel toward the target.

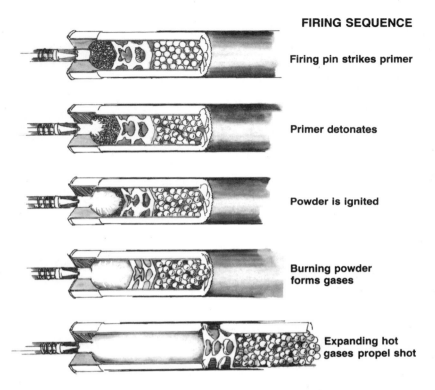

Firing pin strikes primer

Primer detonates

Powder is ignited

Burning powder forms gases

Expanding hot gases propel shot

Because there are different types and sizes of ammunition, an individual who is responsible for safety must understand the functions, types and purposes of each.

CHAPTER 4

CLEANING AND STORAGE

Whether guns are owned for personal protection, hunting, or competition, they operate better when clean and in proper working order. Owners who keep their guns clean and well maintained are also protecting the value of something that usually costs a fair amount of money.

Virtually any mishap that occurs while cleaning guns is not really an "accident," but a failure to apply safety rules. To clean firearms safely, many people apply a simple safety formula based on three factors that must be present before a gun can be fired. The factors are:

> ## Gun + Ammunition + Shooter

Eliminate or separate any one of these factors from the others and a gun cannot be fired. Therefore, in a situation where a gun should not fire — such as during cleaning — simply remove at least one of the factors. This safety formula can be applied to any situation involving guns.

The safety formula applies directly in gun cleaning. By removing at least one of the elements necessary for a gun to be fired, a gun can be cleaned safely. In this case, the element removed is the ammunition. From this concept the following rule is applied:

> ## Ammunition should not be present when cleaning guns.

Cleaning a gun also provides the opportunity to check for proper functioning. If you discover a problem, don't try to fix it yourself; take the gun to a professional gunsmith or return it to the manufacturer for repair.

A clean, properly functioning gun is the safety responsibility of all owners and users.

GUN CLEANING PROCEDURES

To begin cleaning, some basic materials are needed.

- A cleaning rod and bore brush of the correct caliber or gauge and an attachment to hold cleaning patches
- Cloth patches
- Bore cleaning solvent
- Light gun oil
- Small brush
- Clean cloth

Once you have the materials, cleaning is a simple process. The exact steps may vary depending on the type of gun. After ensuring the gun is unloaded and removing any ammunition from the area, follow the steps listed below.

1. Attach the bore brush to the cleaning rod and moisten with solvent. Starting from the breech (rear end) of the barrel, if possible, work the brush back and forth through the bore to loosen residue and fouling. Ensure the brush passes through the bore completely before changing the direction.

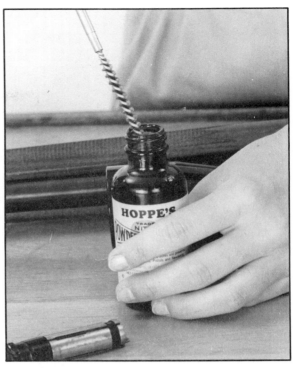

2. Remove the bore brush and attach the cleaning patch to the rod. (Patches come in various sizes so make sure you use the appropriate size.) Run patches through the bore until they come out clean and dry.

3. Push a lightly oiled patch through the bore.

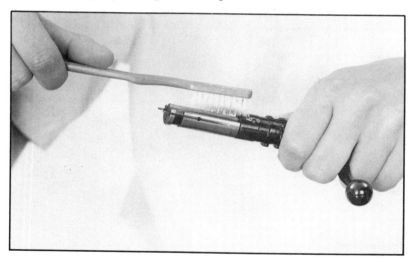

4. Using a small brush or cloth, clean dirt and materials from the gun's action.

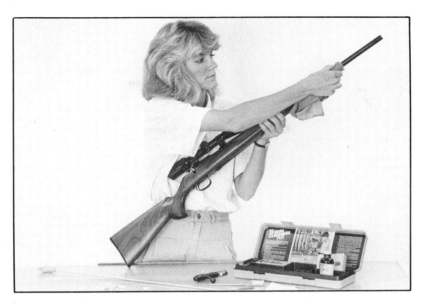

5. Finally, wipe all exposed metal surfaces with a light coat of oil.

STORAGE

Factors such as storage facilities, access by others, personal needs, and security all must be considered when deciding how and where to store guns. However, there is one general rule that *must* be applied under all conditions:

Store guns so they are not accessible to untrained or unauthorized persons.

Answering the following questions will help gun owners evaluate their storage options.

1. What is the gun used for?

A gun stored primarily for personal protection must be ready for immediate use. It may be kept loaded, as long as local laws permit and every precaution is taken to prevent careless or unauthorized individuals from gaining access.

As a general rule, a gun stored for any purpose other than personal protection should never be loaded in the home.

2. How many people live in the home?

A person who lives alone and is trained to handle firearms safely—a police officer, for instance—would need minimal storage precautions. More precautions would be needed if untrained children—or adults—live in the home.

3. Do children in the home know what steps to take if they should find a gun?

Children should be taught to: STOP—DON'T TOUCH; LEAVE THE AREA; TELL AN ADULT.

4. If children in the home have shown an interest in guns, or are learning to handle guns, is qualified adult guidance available?

Firearm safety should be discussed openly and honestly with children who have shown an interest in guns. Parents must not allow children to think firearms are taboo or a mystery that they should investigate on their own.

Once children are mature enough to begin handling guns, they must do so only under qualified adult supervision.

5. Are gun storage facilities in the home adequate?

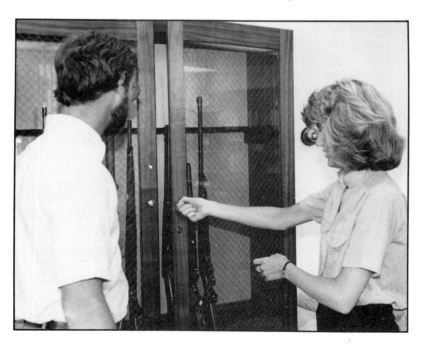

Dozens of secure storage devices such as gun cabinets, wall racks, hard and soft cases, safes and strongboxes are available on the market today. A gun owner considering any of these options should visit a gun shop or study manufacturers' catalogs to choose the most suitable alternative. Some homeowners also store guns in areas of the house, such as attics, for instance, that are not easily accessible.

As a general rule, ammunition should be separated from a firearm storage area and kept in the manufacturer's original box or a strong container that is clearly marked. It should be stored in a cool, dry area, out of reach of untrained or unauthorized individuals.

The proper storage of firearms is the responsibility of all gun owners. Education and the careful consideration of all factors that relate to your individual needs are the key to this responsibility. If you apply the safety formula and the basic safety rules to each situation, a firearm in the home is as safe as any other equipment you may own.

RECORDKEEPING

Many gun owners find it useful to keep a record sheet that describes each firearm stored in the home. The description can be used for insurance purposes, to provide police with information on a stolen gun, or simply when new parts for a firearm need to be ordered. Appendix 2 shows a sample record sheet.

POSTSCRIPT

Gun ownership has been and will continue to be part of American society. Each year millions of Americans, young and old alike, share the unique experiences that the various shooting sports and activities offer.

The choice of being a shooter or not belongs to the individual. The responsibility for safety, however, must be shared by us all. This responsibility begins with education and matures through the development of proper attitudes, knowledge, and skills.

Mastering the information presented in this booklet is the first step toward accepting that responsibility. ALTHOUGH EDUCATION CAN PROVIDE THE ESSENTIALS, APPLYING THIS KNOWLEDGE AND ACCEPTING THE RESPONSIBILITY TOWARD SAFETY ALWAYS REMAINS WITH YOU.

APPENDIX 1

HOW PEOPLE DIED IN HOME ACCIDENTS IN 1988

There were 22,500 accidental deaths in the home and on home premises in 1988. The statistics include death of occupants, guests, trespassers and domestic servants but exclude other persons working on home premises.

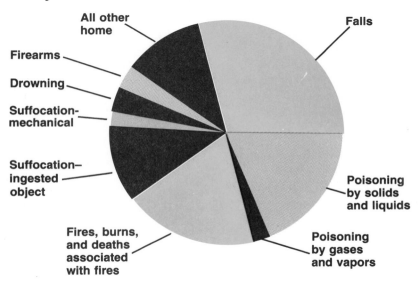

Type	Total	Rate[1]
Falls:	6,500	2.6
Includes deaths from falls one level to another (stairs, ladder, roof, etc.); and on the same level (floor, ground, sidewalk, etc.)		
Poisoning by solids and liquids:	4,300	1.7
Includes deaths from drugs, medicines, mushrooms and shellfish, as well as commonly recognized poisons. Excludes poisonings from spoiled foods, salmonella, etc. —which are classified as disease deaths.		

Fires, burns, and deaths associated with fires: 4,100   1.7
Includes deaths from fires, burns, and from
injuries in conflagrations in the home — such as
asphyxiation, falls and struck by falling objects.
Excludes burns from hot objects or liquids.

Suffocation-ingested object: 2,400   1.0
Includes deaths from accidental ingestion or
inhalation of objects of food resulting in the
obstruction of respiratory passages.

Drowning: 800   0.3
Includes drownings of persons in or on home
premises. Most occur in swimming pools and
bathtubs. Excludes drownings in floods and
other cataclysms.

Firearms: 800   0.3
Includes firearm accidents in or on home
premises. Many occur while cleaning or playing
with guns. Excludes deaths from explosive
materials.

Poisoning by gases and vapors: 600   0.2
Principally carbon monoxide due to incomplete
combustion, involving cooking stoves, heating
equipment and standing motor vehicles. Gas
poisonings in conflagrations are classified as
fire deaths.

Suffocation-mechanical: 500   0.2
Includes deaths from smothering bed clothes,
thin plastic materials, etc., suffocation by
cave-ins or confinement in closed spaces, and
mechanical strangulation.

All other home: 2,500   1.0
Most important types included are: electric
current, explosive materials, hot substance,
corrosive liquid, and steam.

---

[1] Deaths per 100,000 population.

Source: *Accident Facts*, 1989 edition, publication of the National Safety
Council.

HOW PEOPLE DIED IN PUBLIC ACCIDENTS IN 1988

There were 67,000 public accidental deaths including deaths in public places or places used in a public way, including motor vehicles. Most sports and recreation deaths are included. Excludes deaths in the course of employment.

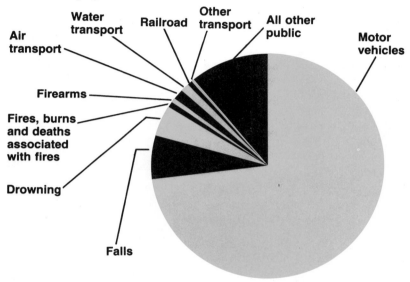

Type	Total	Rate[1]
Motor vehicles: Includes deaths involving mechanically or electrically powered highway-transport vehicles in motion (except those on rails) both on and off the highway or street.	49,000	19.9
Falls: Includes deaths from falls in public places. Excludes deaths in falls from moving vehicles.	4,100	1.7
Drowning: Includes drownings of persons swimming or playing in water, or falling into water, except on home premises or at work. Excludes drownings involving boats, which are in water transportation.	2,900	1.2

Air transport:	900	0.4
Includes deaths in private flying, passengers in commercial aviation, and deaths of military personnel in accidents in the U.S. Excludes crews and persons traveling in the course of employment.		
Water transport:	800	0.3
Includes deaths in water transport accidents from falls, burns, etc., as well as drownings. More than nine out of ten of the drownings involved occupants of small boats.		
Fires, burns, and deaths associated with fires:	600	0.2
Includes deaths from fires, burns and injuries in conflagrations in public places such as asphyxiation, falls and struck by falling objects. Excludes burns from hot objects or liquids.		
Firearms:	500	0.2
Includes deaths from firearm accidents in public places, including hunting accidents. Excludes deaths from explosive materials.		
Railroad:	300	0.1
Includes deaths arising from railroad vehicles in motion (except those involving motor vehicles), subway and elevated trains, persons boarding or alighting from standing trains.		
Other transport:	200	0.1
Includes deaths in accidents involving pedal-cycles, animal-drawn vehicles, street cars, etc., except in collision with motor vehicles. Excludes trolley buses, subways, elevateds, scooters.		
All other public:	7,700	3.1
Most important types included are: medical complications, excessive heat or cold, suffocation by ingestion, and poisoning by solid and liquid.		

[1] Deaths per 100,000 population.

Source: *Accident Facts*, 1989 edition, publication of the National Safety Council.

Year	Motor Vehicles	Falls	Drown-ing[b]
1903-1912 avg.	1,200	(a)	9,030
1913-1922 avg.	9,750	13,870	8,110
1923-1932 avg.	26,510	16,660	7,590
1933-1942 avg.	34,931	22,258	6,730
1943-1952 avg.	31,577	22,667	6,598
1953-1962 avg.	38,222	19,575	6,483(c)
1963-1972 avg.	52,234	18,535	7,193
1973	55,511	16,506	8,725
1974	46,402	16,339	7,876
1975	45,853	14,896	8,000
1976	47,038	14,136	6,827
1977	49,510	13,773	7,126
1978	52,411	13,690	7,026
1979	53,524	13,216	6,872
1980	53,172	13,294	7,257
1981	51,385	12,628	6,277
1982	45,779	12,077	6,351
1983	44,452	12,024	6,353
1984	46,263	11,937	5,388
1985	45,901	12,001	5,316
1986	47,865	11,444	5,700
1987	48,400	11,400	5,400
1988	49,000	12,000	5,000
			Changes
1978 to 1988	-7%	-12%	-29%

ACCIDENTAL DEATHS

TO 1988

Fires, Burns[d]	Ingest. of Food, Object	Fire-arms	Poison (Solid, Liquid)	Poison by Gas
9,110	(a)	2,070	(a)	(a)
8,100	(a)	2,500	2,980	(a)
7,215	(a)	2,980	2,620	2,660
7,382	(a)	2,703	2,003	1,593
6,816(e)	1,187	2,358	1,730	1,811
6,776(c)	1,973(c)	2,230	1,538	1,211
7,311	2,473	2,425	2,773	1,563
6,503	3,013	2,618	3,683	1,652
6,236	2,991	2,513	4,016	1,518
6,071	3,106	2,380	4,694	1,577
6,338	3,033	2,059	4,161	1,569
6,357	3,037	1,982	3,374	1,596
6,163	3,063	1,806	3,035	1,737
5,991	3,243	2,004	3,165	1,472
5,822	3,249	1,955	3,089	1,242
5,697	3,331	1,871	3,243	1,280
5,210	3,254	1,756	3,474	1,259
5,028	3,387	1,695	3,382	1,251
5,010	3,541	1,668	3,808	1,103
4,938	3,551	1,649	4,091	1,079
4,835	3,692	1,452	4,731	1,009
5,000	3,400	1,300	4,600	1,000
5,000	3,600	1,400	5,300	1,000

in Deaths

-19%	+18%	-22%	+75%	-42%

Year	Motor Vehicles	Falls	Drown-ing[b]
1903-1912 avg.	1.6	(a)	10.3
1913-1922 avg.	9.3	13.4	7.7
1923-1932 avg.	22.1	13.9	6.3
1933-1942 avg.	26.9	17.2	5.2
1943-1952 avg.	21.8	15.8	4.6
1953-1962 avg.	22.2	11.4	3.8(c)
1963-1972 avg.	26.3	9.4	3.6
1973	26.3	7.8	4.1
1974	21.8	7.7	3.7
1975	21.3	6.9	3.7
1976	21.6	6.5	3.1
1977	22.5	6.3	3.2
1978	23.6	6.2	3.2
1979	23.8	5.9	3.1
1980	23.4	5.9	3.2
1981	22.4	5.5	2.7
1982	19.7	5.2	2.7
1983	19.0	5.1	2.7
1984	19.6	5.0	2.3
1985	19.2	5.0	2.2
1986	19.9	4.7	2.4
1987	19.9	4.7	2.2
1988	19.9	4.9	2.0
			Changes
1978 to 1988	-16%	-21%	-38%

Source: National Center for Health Statistics and National Safety Council.

(a) Comparable data not available.
(b) Includes drowning in water transport accidents.

100,000 POPULATION

Fires, Burns[d]	Ingest. of Food, Object	Fire- arms	Poison (Solid, Liquid)	Poison by Gas
(a)	(a)	2.4	(a)	(a)
8.8	(a)	2.4	2.8	(a)
7.0	(a)	2.5	2.2	2.2
5.6	(a)	2.1	1.5	1.2
5.2	0.8	1.6	1.1	1.3
4.0(c)	1.1(c)	1.3	0.9	0.7
3.7	1.3	1.2	1.4	0.8
3.1	1.4	1.2	1.7	0.8
2.9	1.4	1.2	1.8	0.7
2.8	1.4	1.1	2.2	0.7
2.9	1.4	0.9	1.9	0.7
2.9	1.4	0.9	1.5	0.7
2.8	1.4	0.8	1.4	0.8
2.7	1.4	0.9	1.4	0.7
2.6	1.4	0.9	1.4	0.5
2.5	1.5	0.8	1.4	0.6
2.2	1.4	0.8	1.4	0.5
2.1	1.4	0.7	1.4	0.5
2.1	1.5	0.7	1.6	0.5
2.1	1.5	0.7	1.7	0.5
2.0	1.5	0.6	2.0	0.4
2.1	1.4	0.5	1.9	0.4
2.0	1.5	0.6	2.2	0.4

in Rates

-29%	+ 7%	-25%	+57%	-50%

(c) Data are not comparable to previous years shown due to classification changes in 1958 and 1968.

(d) Includes burns by fire, and deaths resulting from conflagration regardless of nature of injury.

APPENDIX 2: FIREARM RECORD SHEET

Keeping a record sheet for each of your firearms is useful. Should a gun be stolen, the police will need the most complete description of it you can provide. (A clear photograph of the gun will be helpful as well.) The information can also be used for insurance records or submitted to a manufacturer in case you ever need to order parts for the gun. File record sheets with other important papers.

Type

      Rifle_____ Shotgun_____ Handgun_____

Manufacturer _____ Model _____

Serial # _____ Action _____

Caliber _____ Special Features _____

Purchase Cost _____ Estimated Value _____

APPENDIX 3: GUN SAFETY CHECKLIST

1. Do you have a gun in the home?   Yes   No

2. Is the gun inaccessible to unauthorized people
    (including children)?   Yes   No

3. What gun storage options do you utilize:
    Wall rack   Gun cabinet
    Strongbox   Hard or soft case
    Gun safe   Other

4. Is the gun kept unloaded unless actually being used
    for personal protection?   Yes   No

5. Do you know how to open the action to check that
    your gun is unloaded?   Yes   No

6. Is ammunition correctly identified and securely
    stored separately from the gun?   Yes   No

7. Have all muzzleloading firearms in your home
    been checked to ensure they are unloaded?   Yes   No

8. If black powder is kept in your home, is it stored
    in a cool dry area and in its original container?   Yes   No

9. Do members of your family understand the three
    fundamental rules of gun safety?   Yes   No

10. Do young children in your home know what steps
    to take if they should find a gun?   Yes   No

11. Do all members of your family recognize that air
    guns are not toys and should be treated like all
    other guns?   Yes   No

12. Have members of your family who shoot taken a
    course in firearm safety and marksmanship?   Yes   No

13. Have you located a knowledgeable person who
    can answer questions you may have on firearms
    or firearm safety?   Yes   No

14. Are you familiar with federal, state, and local
    laws pertaining to possession, storage and trans-
    portation of firearms within your community?   Yes   No

APPENDIX 4

HOME FIREARM SAFETY REVIEW

A. Identify the following parts of a gun.

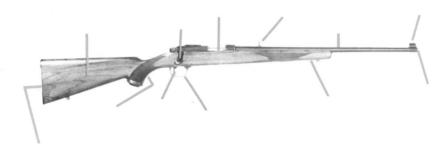

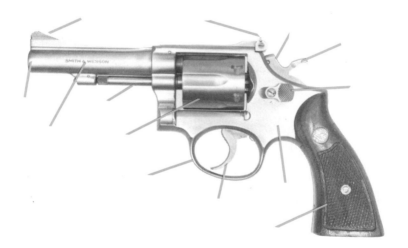

B. Completion

   1. What are the two main causes of gun accidents?

2. List the three primary rules for safe gun handling.

3. What is the most important safe gun handling rule? Why is this so important?

4. What is the main consideration when storing a gun?

C. Multiple choice. Circle *all* the correct answers.

    1. If you do not know how to operate a gun, you should:

        a. Read the owner's manual.

        b. Take it to a gun dealer.

        c. Have a trained person look at it.

        d. Not touch it.

2. How do you check to see if a gun is unloaded?

    a. Pull the trigger.

    b. Remove or empty the magazine as appropriate; open and visually check the action.

    c. Look down the barrel and visually check.

3. What are some safe storage options?

    a. Hard or soft cases

    b. Cabinets

    c. Safes

    d. Wall-mounted racks

4. What should be considered when storing guns and ammunition?

    a. Dryness of storage area

    b. Heat

    c. Intended use

    d. Accessibility

5. What should you do if you suspect a muzzleloading firearm is loaded?

    a. Fire it.

    b. Leave it alone.

    c. Have a qualified person inspect it.

    d. Try to remove the ammunition.

D. True or False—Mark whether the statement is true or false. If the statement is false, correct it.

    1. The main difference between a rifle and a shotgun is appearance.

2. The action is the moving parts that allow you to load, fire and unload the gun.

3. A gun in good condition can simply fire.

4. Guns stored in the home should be accessible only to trained, authorized individuals.

5. Most ammunition is compatible with all types of guns.

6. A gun should be kept unloaded except when ready for use.

7. It is okay to rest your finger on the trigger as long as you don't pull it.

8. Shotguns fire "shot," which are round projectiles usually made of lead or steel.

9. Since the 1940s the number of firearm accidents has been decreasing.

10. Never smoke around black powder or primers.

11. A firearm is simply a device that holds, aims and fires ammunition.

APPENDIX 5:

RESOURCES

1. **NRA Certified Instructors.** The National Rifle Association has more than 26,000 certified instructors who teach gun safety and basic marksmanship skills to the general public. If after reading this book you have questions or desire to learn more, contact a local instructor. For a listing of local instructors write: NRA Instructor/Coach Programs Department, 1600 Rhode Island Avenue, N.W., Washington, D.C. 20036.

2. **NRA Affiliated Clubs.** There are more than 13,000 clubs affiliated with NRA. Clubs are formed by people who share a common interest in gun safety and shooting activities. Some clubs are specialized: hunting, rifle, pistol, trap or skeet. For a listing of clubs in your area, write: NRA Clubs and Associations Department, 1600 Rhode Island Avenue, N.W., Washington, D.C. 20036.

3. **NRA State Associations**. Each state, Puerto Rico and the District of Columbia have NRA designated state associations, responsible for supporting and promoting all aspects of the shooting sports. They sponsor state NRA sanctioned competitions; promote programs that expand junior involvement in the shooting sports; administer the Director of Civilian Marksmanship program; and monitor firearms/hunting legislation in their states. Contact the NRA Clubs and Associations Department for more information about your state association.

4. **NRA Field Representatives**. NRA has 21 Field Representatives across the country who represent the NRA national office in their respective area. They provide membership assistance, help clubs develop and implement NRA programs, grant media interviews, attend competitive shooting events as NRA officials and provide assistance in planning and building of shooting ranges. To locate the Field Representative for your area, call (202) 828-6126.

5. **Materials**. There are many references that supplement the safety information in this book. To order listed materials, contact the NRA Sales Department at 1-800-336-7402 in the continental United States except Virginia. Residents of Virginia, Hawaii and Alaska call 1-703-683-8666, ext. 240. Please note that the listed prices do not include shipping or handling fees.

	Item #	Cost
Books—Safety and Use		
The Basics of Rifle Shooting	EF5N1059	$ 3.50
The Basics of Shotgun Shooting	EF5N3057	$ 2.00
The Muzzleloading Rifle Handbook	EZ5N1059	$ 2.00
The Muzzleloading Shotgun Handbook	EZ5N3057	$ 2.00
The Muzzleloading Pistol Handbook	EZ5N2058	$ 2.00
The Basics of Personal Protection	ES5N2061	$ 2.00
NRA Junior Rifle Shooting Handbook	EM5N1055	$ 3.00
Pamphlets		
At Home With Guns	ES3N0136	NC
A Parent's Guide to Gun Safety	ES3N0145	NC
Eddie Eagle Safety Coloring Book	ES3N1108	NC
Eddie Eagle Safety Coloring Book (Set of 50)	ES5N1115	$10.00
Safe Gun Handling Brochure	ES3N0010	NC
Shooting For Safety— (BB Gun Safety Brochure)	ES3N2303	NC
Firearms Safety in the Field (Hunting)	HI3N0099	NC
David's First Hunt Coloring Book	HI5N5001	$ 0.75
Videotapes		
Rifle Shooting Fundamentals		
(VHS)	EF5N1531	$35.00
(BETA)	EF5N1522	
Pistol Shooting Fundamentals		
(VHS)	EF5N2530	$30.00
(BETA)	EF5N2521	
Shotgun Shooting Fundamentals		
(VHS)	EF5N3539	$30.00
(BETA)	EF5N3520	
A Woman's Guide to Firearms		
(VHS)	ES5N3506	$34.95
(BETA)	ES5N3551	
Principles of Home Defense		
(VHS)	ES5N2409	$29.95
(BETA)	ES5N2454	
Other		
The Parent's Safety Kit	ES5N0625	$ 5.00

—Using the message: Stop—Don't Touch—Leave the Area—Tell

an Adult, this kit is designed to help parents teach their young children (kindergarten–6th grade) to be safe around guns. It contains "A Parent's Guide to Gun Safety" brochure; instructional guidelines; Eddie Eagle Safety Poster; two coloring books; two sets of coloring sheets and activity sheets; and discussion questions.

Eddie Eagle Safety Poster	ES5N0410	$ 2.00
Safe Gun Handling Poster	ES5N5255	$ 2.00
NRA Firearms Fact Book	PB1N0097	$ 9.95

APPENDIX 6:

ANSWER KEY

A.

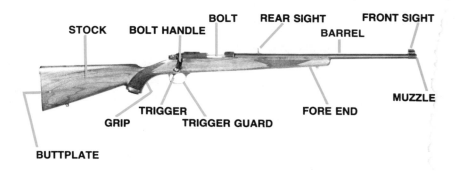

STOCK · BOLT HANDLE · BOLT · REAR SIGHT · BARREL · FRONT SIGHT · MUZZLE · FORE END · TRIGGER · TRIGGER GUARD · GRIP · BUTTPLATE

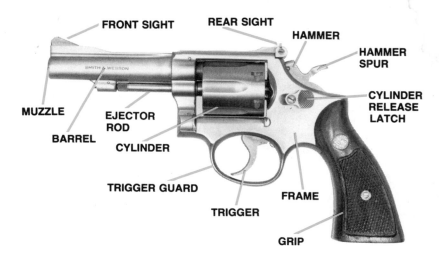

FRONT SIGHT · REAR SIGHT · HAMMER · HAMMER SPUR · CYLINDER RELEASE LATCH · MUZZLE · EJECTOR ROD · BARREL · CYLINDER · TRIGGER GUARD · FRAME · TRIGGER · GRIP

B.

   1. Carelessness and lack of knowledge.

69

2. Always keep the gun pointed in a safe direction. Always keep your finger off the trigger until ready to shoot. Always keep the gun unloaded until ready to use.

3. Always keep the gun pointed in a safe direction. Even if the gun is fired, no one should be injured if the gun is pointed in a safe direction.

4. Store guns so they are not accessible to unauthorized persons.

C.

1. a,c,d. Do not transport a gun if you are not sure how it is operated or if it is loaded.

2. b only. Never pull the trigger unless you intend to fire the gun at a particular object. Looking down the barrel puts your face in front of the muzzle, violating the golden rule of safety, and will not tell you if the gun is loaded.

3. a,b,c,d

4. a,b,c,d

5. b and c. Under no circumstances should an untrained individual attempt to unload a firearm himself.

D.

1. False. It may be difficult for a non-shooter to distinguish a rifle from a shotgun. The main difference between a rifle and a shotgun is their ammunition.

2. True

3. False. A gun in good condition **cannot** simply go off. It takes human involvement.

4. True

5. False. Ammunition comes in specific sizes and must be compatible with the gun.

6. True

7. False. That could lead to an accident! Only put your finger on the trigger when you are ready to fire it.

8. True. Shotguns may also shoot "slugs"—a single projectile.

9. True

10. True

11. True